RAV DOVBER PINSON

THE JEWISH WEDDING

A GUIDE TO THE RITUALS AND TRADITIONS
OF THE WEDDING CEREMONY

בס"ד

Dear Guests,

With tremendous gratitude to Hashem and hearts filled to the brim with joy, we welcome you to participate in this great occasion.

The day of a person's wedding is the most auspicious and significant day of that person's life and it is our honor to share this day with all of you gathered with us today.

In Judaism, marriage is not simply viewed as the joining of two people with similar interests, attractions and shared life goals. It is seen as the joining of souls, and a shared life *Tikkun*/purpose.

"It is not good for man to be alone." These words were spoken at the very beginning of the human existence. Existentially, we are meant to go through life with a partner. This makes our life more large, meaningful and beyond our egoistic needs and desires.

On a spiritual realm, there are souls that are meant to be together, and through the process of dating and self-discovery one finds that person who is predestined to be their partner in life.

"There is no joy like the resolution of doubt," and the finding of one's soul mate is the rediscovery of a part of one's self that has been missing until now. This is part of the tremendous joy that we celebrate on the wedding day.

The blessing we offer to a bride and groom is to build a "*Bayit ne'eman b'yisrael*/An everlasting edifice in the House of Israel."

This home that is being built by the new couple is one in a long chain of loving, committed marriages and homes that have made up the unbroken chain of our ancestry and—G-d willing—future generations. For this reason, it is said that previous generations of ancestors join in spirit under the *Chuppah*, because this union is so much larger than just the two souls who have found each other. This union solidifies and continues the chain of Jewish life, and is the greatest *Nachat*/spiritual pleasure that the souls above can experience.

As the epicenter of Jewish life and continuity for millennia, there are myriads of rituals, customs and traditions interwoven into the wedding ceremony and celebration. We hope this guide will introduce you to some of the lesser known and enlighten you further to those you may already be aware of. Ancient and modern, these deeply meaningful and beautiful rituals are meant to open us up to an awareness of the magnitude of the moment.

Our sincere hope is that this guide will encourage you to be more than a spectator at this wedding. You and all our honored guests are active participants celebrating with us together in a most profound and meaningful manner, opening ourselves up to the experience of wonder and joy that this occasion elicits.

Enjoy, and Mazal Tov!

Rabbi Dovber and Rochie Pinson

This guide is based on the teachings of Torah, Talmud, Medrash, Zohar, Halacha, Poskim, Kabbalah, Chassidus, and writings culled from the seven Chabad Rebbeim. By quoting their teachings we actively draw down the 'presence' of these holy souls who revealed these teachings, thus extending blessings to the bride and groom and all in attendance.

KABBALAT PANIM
Welcoming the Guests

T

The wedding begins with the *Kabbalat Panim*/receiving the guests.
Two areas or rooms are prepared. One area for the *Chatan*/groom,
and one for the *Kallah*/bride.

A bride and groom on the day of their wedding are likened to a queen and king.
Both the bride and groom sit in the middle of their respective rooms—
usually the bride's chair is decorated and enhanced with flowers, like a throne for a queen—
and people come to greet them and be greeted by them.

The attendees approach the bride and groom to wish *Mazal Tov*
and offer their blessings, and in turn, the bride and groom bless all the guests.

The demeanor of the wedding, from the Kabbalat Panim until immediately after the Chuppah,
is somewhat solemn and sober. Our sages tell us that on the day of a person's wedding
all their sins and mistakes are forgiven. It is a day similar to Yom Kippur,
a day of introspection and forgiveness, and as such, the common practice is for the
bride and groom, and sometimes even their parents, to fast on the day of the wedding,
until after the Chuppah, as they would on Yom Kippur.

WORDS OF TORAH

The groom holds court and sits with family and friends at the table, often referred to as the "*Tish*" (Yiddish for table). The custom is for the groom to publicly share words of Torah. At some point, whether in the middle of him speaking, or once concluded and started over again (just for effect!), the crowd cheers and 'interrupts him' much like the cheering of the crowds when a king would talk. The words of Torah he shares are usually related to the theme of a wedding.

The Chabad custom is to recite a *Ma'amar*/ a Chassidic, mystical discourse on the spiritual nature of a wedding, addressing the cosmic and microcosmic aspects of the day.

THE TENA'IM/AGREEMENT

At the Kabbalat Panim, in the groom's side of the party, the *Tena'im* are signed and read aloud. The tena'im is a contract of agreement, in which the two parties commit to marry each other.

The tena'im contract begins with the words, *"To good fortune. May [this match] flourish and grow like a verdant garden."* This is an acknowledgment that marriage needs watering; it is the garden of life, one that will hopefully produce beautiful fruit, in children and good deeds, but a marriage, like a garden, needs constant tending with careful attention and care.

BREAKING A PLATE

Following the commitment and signing, the tena'im are read aloud and then the mothers of the bride and groom (or closest female relatives in the absence of mothers) break an earthenware plate.

This irreversible act of breaking the plate represents the finality of the tena'im, the sealing of the commitment.

Metaphorically, just as a shattered plate is final and forever, we are declaring and blessing the bride and groom that the marriage should be ever-lasting, a permanent edifice and a union for life.

Symbolically, an earthenware pot or dish serves as an intermediary between the fire underneath and the water within. Like fire and water, a bride and groom are opposites and often need help to be brought together to the chuppah.

The plate symbolizes that which brought them together—whether it was a matchmaker, a friend or the parents—and as we shatter the plate, we acknowledge that this assistance is no longer needed and the chuppah will now merge the two, without any further interface or interference required.

Excitement builds as music fills the space, and the groom begins to walk toward his bride. Arms linked with his parents, or with father and father-in-law, the groom is led by a procession of his friends and family to where the bride awaits, in her seat of honor.

The Chabad tradition is to begin singing the holiest of tunes at this moment.

The "*Daled Bavot*"/Four movements, is a *Nigun*, or wordless melody, composed by the holy Alter Rebbe, the first Chabad Rebbe. The tune is sung from the deepest part of our soul, and connects us to the composer himself, drawing down his presence into this holy assembly. As the Tzemach Tzedek taught, for this reason when singing a song of a Rebbe, we should imagine the image of the Tzadik in front of us.

This tune will continue to be sung as the bride and groom walk towards the chuppah.

The bride and groom have not seen each other for seven days. This is the moment they rediscover each other, as bride and groom. The longing, excitement and anticipation is intense. While surrounded and accompanied by family and friends, this is also a deeply private and personal moment for the bride and groom.

The groom, led by the procession, approaches his bride and lovingly covers her face with a veil. The act of covering the bride, is reminiscent of our foremother Rivka, who veiled her face upon catching a glimpse of her future husband Yitzchak for the very first time.

Marriage is a union of body and soul. Attraction plays an integral role is moving the potential couple towards each other, but ultimately, marriage is far more than a physical union; it is a union of souls, shared dreams, aspirations, hopes and longings.

On the deepest level, marriage is an awareness of a shared singular soul purpose. Attraction to the external beauty of one's spouse is essential, but not the sole reason for the attraction, as there is a sense of deeper connection that transcends externality. Externality fades, but inner beauty never does.

By the act of veiling, and thus no longer seeing each other's faces, the groom and the bride are declaring that they are marrying each other for reasons that extend far beyond the external and superficial appearance of the other. The hiddenness of the face declares; "I will love, cherish and respect you for who you truly are; on a soul level. The self that you have revealed to me, and even the parts of self that you have not yet revealed, or maybe cannot ever reveal; I am marrying all of you."

THE MARRIAGE CEREMONY
Under the Chuppah

PREPARING

Following the Badeken, the bride and groom each prepare themselves for the chuppah. All jewelry is removed and all knots are untied, such as shoelaces or neckties.

There are simple *Halachic*/technical reasons for these customs, but on a symbolic level, the removal of all jewelry suggests that the couple is entering into the marriage not for any financial gain, and the untying of all knots implies a certain type of freedom and relinquishing of all former ties and all forms of things that may hold one back from entering into a lasting relationship. The couple can now, freely and with openness, love and mutual respect, be bound with each other in the eternal bond of marriage.

Symbolically, the removal of all ornaments and jewelry is similar to the *Kohen Gadol*/High Priest who entered the Holy of Holies of the *Beis HaMikdash*/Temple on Yom Kippur with the simplest of white garments, as the Holy of Holies is the place of true *Yichud*/Unity.

THE KITTEL

Customarily, the groom wears a *Kittel* – a white frock, like the one worn on Yom Kippur, for the chuppah. There is a custom to wear the kittel under an overcoat, so as to be less ostentatious. Both the bride and groom are wearing white. White represents purity, potential, before the various colors of life are painted in. On Yom Kippur we also dress in white or with a kittel, reflecting the idea of new beginnings.

Today is the personal Yom Kippur of the bride and groom, and their white garments reflect that they are entering into the marriage with purity and openness. They step into the covenant of marriage with a sense of newness, and beginning with a clean slate.

White reflects the entire spectrum of visible colors. White thus represents the backdrop of reality, upon which all shades and colors of life are projected. Our souls, our innermost purity, is the backdrop of our manifest self. White is the soul connection, representing the 'empty' infinite space where these two souls are unified as one.

Getting married in white represents a commitment that no matter the shades and colors that may be projected throughout life, the bride and groom are connected on a soul level where all is pure and possible.

THE CHUPPAH

A chuppah is a canopy or covered area resting on four poles, or columns. Some people use an heirloom talit, of a grandparent or parent, as the cover of the canopy.

Halachically, the chuppah constitutes a private domain, the four columns representing the image of the chuppah as a defined 'square' space. When the bride joins the groom under the chuppah's covering, it is another step towards the finalization of the marriage.

Although covered and a square space with defined boundaries, the chuppah has no walls and is open on all four sides. This symbolizes the home the bride and groom are committed to establish, a place of shelter, and yet, as the tent of Avraham and Sarah, one that is open on all sides for all guests to enter. This is a commitment to create an island in space, but still a space that is open to others.

A common custom is to place the chuppah under the open skies. The foundation of the marriage is based on the "heavens," meaning lofty ideals and aspiration.

Additionally, this recalls Hashem's blessing to Avraham, that his offspring will be as numerous as the stars of the sky.

Under the skies is also symbolic of the infinite expanse. "The sky's the limit." Under the sky represents a place of infinite potential.

The *Ohr*/Divine Light that is revealed at the chuppah is an *Ohr Makif*/Transcendent Surrounding Light of blessings and flow, as the AriZal teaches. All the physical blessings of this future marriage, for health, prosperity, children, peace and so forth, is all drawn down at the chuppah.

The Miteler Rebbe writes that this is also true of the spiritual blessings. All the spiritual, mental and emotional work that the bride and groom will achieve throughout their future lives together is drawn down at the chuppah.

As the couple ties an eternal bond, they are linked to the generations past and G-d willing, to all future generations, as they connect to the highest and deepest Infinite Ohr of Makif.

As a time of eternity and infinity, souls of our loved ones who have passed on—deceased parents, grandparents and great-grandparents of the bride and groom—are spiritually present at the chuppah.

Individual people become linked in unity under the chuppah, and together, they are connected to the collective eternal people of *Klal Yisrael*/People of Israel.

At a chuppah there are often many tears shed. These are tears that flow from deep prayer, longing, and a strong desire to draw down all the blessings for the couple in their future lives at this tremendously joyful and momentous time.

On their wedding day, the bride and groom are considered to be *Tzadikim*, holy and righteous. A traditional custom is to ask the bride and groom to pray for us under the chuppah, with the awareness that their prayers at this moment are most powerful and heard.

SEVEN CIRCLES

The groom approaches the chuppah first, to await the arrival of his bride. He is led by an entourage of parents and grandparents, all supporting him and guiding him towards his future.

The procession walks to the chuppah carrying candles, as a reminder of the light and fire of Mount Sinai, when we all collectively entered into a marriage with the Creator.

The bride—as queen—is the main event, and she arrives last. She is also led by her parents, or her mother and mother-in-law, as each family's custom dictates, and of course, the grandparents, who are part of the procession as well. All rise to greet her as she enters.

As the bride enters into the space of the chuppah, she and her escorts begin to circle the groom seven times. As she circles, she is creating. Just as creation occurred in seven days, the bride is now creating a new reality, and with seven circles she brings her new creation of this unique marriage to a place of completion and wholeness.

Mystically, circles represent infinity, a place of no beginning and no end. In this way, a circle embodies the quality of *Makif*, the transcendent encircling Infinite Light that is revealed at the chuppah and the quality of Makif that the bride brings to the groom. This is the reason for the custom that a man only begins using a *talit*, representing Ohr Makif, after his wedding ceremony.

Defined squares, such as the chuppah, represent a place of law, boundaries and limits. The bride and groom enter into the square space of the chuppah to draw strict boundaries within the marriage. And yet, there must always be the circles within the marriage, the place of poetry and passion, and therefore we create circles within the square of the chuppah.

It begins with the bride encircling the groom, and later with the groom encircling a ring on his bride.

As the bride circles the groom, she is "marking her territory," and weaving around the groom a pattern of protection. Encircling creates a sacred space within and creates a boundary and protection from everything that is outside that sacred circle. There are seven dominant emotional and interpersonal attributes, the emotional *Sefirot*. With each circle drawn, the bride is drawing down each of these positive attributes into her marriage, and excluding its negative counterpart.

For example, the first circle corresponds to the attribute of *Chesed*/giving and openness. By encircling, the bride is laying the foundations of a relationship that will be established on a base of love, openness and generosity. Simultaneously, she is shutting out all infringing, false love and unhealthy attachments. The second circle is analogous to the attribute of *Gevurah*/strength, judgment, discipline and boundaries. The bride circles, and is laying a foundation for the marriage that is solid with positive respect for each other's space and healthy boundaries while excluding all forms of negative judgment or lack of boundaries. And each of the circles continues this way, laying down layers of positive emotional sefirot into the relationship.

THE BLESSINGS

Many have a custom to call upon all the Kohanim present, or a single elder Kohen to offer the priestly blessings of G-dly grace and peace to the couple and by extension to all the wedding guests.

The officiating Rabbi or an elder Rabbi is customarily invited to address the bride and groom at this point, and offer them his blessings.

The Chabad custom these days is to read the letter of blessings that the Rebbe would send to a bride and groom. The words of the righteous are eternal, and echoing these words today manifests these very same blessings from on High.

THE KIDDUSHIN

The *Kiddushin* is the actual betrothal through the ring ceremony, initiated by the blessing over the marriage.

A cup of wine is filled to the brim, as in every joyful ceremonial moment in Judaism, and the officiating Rabbi recites a blessing over the wine and a blessing over the betrothal.

This blessing over the marriage is both a *Birchat HaMitzvot*/blessing for the Mitzvah of marriage and also a *Birchat Hoda'ah*/a thanksgiving blessing, thanking Hashem for this awesome moment.

THE RING

After the blessing the wine is consumed.

For the marriage to be established, the groom gives the bride a gift that is worth a significant sum. According to a custom that goes back hundreds of years, the gift that is given is a simple gold ring which the groom places on the bride's finger.

Taba'at/ring is numerically 481, as is the word kiddushin. The ring is placed on the index finger, which is the seventh finger, to represent creation, which occurred in seven days, at this moment.

The ring is a circle, connected to the circular theme of marriage, and symbolic of the bride and groom entering into a new circle of life. The bride previously encircled the groom, and the Rebbe writes that by giving the ring, the groom is metaphorically circling the bride, and together they stand under a round sky and the Light of Makif and the *Shechina*/Divine Presence.

Before the groom places the ring on his bride, he declares in front of two witnesses,

"הרי את מקודשת לי בטבעת זו כדת משה וישראל"

"With this ring, you are consecrated to me according to the law of Moshe and Israel" and then places the ring on her finger.

Mazal Tov, the couple are now betrothed!
At this point, the *Ketubah*, the Halachic marriage contract, is read aloud and handed to the groom who gives it to the bride for safekeeping.

SHEVA BERACHOT/ SEVEN BLESSINGS

The seven blessings are now recited and with it, the finalization of the marriage ceremony.

Seven once again, as the theme of the chuppah, symbolizing the new creation of this marriage and the joining of two individuals in a sacred bond of unity.

All the blessings speak about the wonderful possibilities of marriage and love. We bless the couple that their love and the home that they build together should shine brightly and be bathed in the light of the Garden of Eden and the delight of Adam and Eve in the purest place of unity and perfection.

BREAKING THE CUP

The marriage ceremony concludes with the breaking of a glass.

This is a time of profound joy on an individual level, and yet we still acknowledge the destruction of the Temple and the collective exile, the fact that the world is still broken and incomplete.

In this broken world we are all still imperfect, and there is alienation and distance that can occur, yet the beauty and healing of this marriage is that despite the brokenness and imperfection, we see the beauty and wholeness in our spouse. In marriage itself, there is occasionally a shattering, but we collectively shout "Mazel Tov" upon the breaking of the glass, to bless all the future brokenness with healing.

When these two people commit to each other with love and respect, they continuously build, and rebuild, even after brokenness, and together build up the "desolate places of Jerusalem," bringing the world closer to the ultimate redemption.

There were two sets of *Luchot*/Tablets. The first set was given to all of us at Sinai, with great commotion and spectacular pomp. This set was eventually broken. Then we were given the second set quietly, privately and modestly. This set survived. The breaking of the glass reminds us of the broken tablets, and it is reminding the newlyweds that what matters most in a marriage is not the outward show, the appearance, but what occurs in the quietness of the home, when no one is around except your spouse. And it is these private moments of intimacy that is most important and what creates ever-lasting relationships.

Breaking the glass, much like the breaking of the plate earlier in the ceremony, suggests an ending, a solidifying of the marriage contract. Once the cup is broken, we joyfully shout "Mazal Tov."

For something radically new to occur, there needs to be a shattering of the old. While the bride and groom are eager to begin their new life together, there is a certain sadness in the ending of their previous lives as singles.

Growth requires a letting go of the old form and function, and the shattering of the glass symbolizes this. We are making space for a new life, a life shared with another in love, vulnerability, respect and mutual growth to begin at this very moment.

THE YICHUD ROOM

Joyfully, accompanied by music and festivity, the new couple is escorted to the *Yichud*/unity room, where they will spend sometime alone in privacy, before reemerging as a brand new couple to join the celebration.

Traditionally, in the Yichud room they will also break their wedding day fast and eat their first meal together as a married couple. The Yichud room is an extension of the chuppah, a private space for the couple to truly be alone and unified.

THE CELEBRATION
Reception and Dancing

With great pomp and ceremony, the bride and groom are introduced as a married couple, and welcomed into the hall with music and dancing.

To bring joy to the bride and groom is a lofty and special Mitzvah. We bring joy to the new couple by praising them to each other in our toasts and speeches and of course, through participating in the dancing and festivities with full hearts!

It is a long-standing tradition, dating back to Talmudic times, to lift the bride and groom—each on their respective side of the mechitzah—on chairs or on our shoulders and dance with them held aloft.

Lifting and dancing suggests a type of elevation, writes the Alter Rebbe, raising the bride and groom beyond the world of the immediate and tapping into the world of *Makif*, higher, deeper, surrounding Light.

In general, there is a certain elevation that occurs with dancing as we lift our feet off the ground. Yet, on the other hand, dancing happens with our very physical bodies, clapping with our hands and stamping with our feet. The Rebbe Rashab writes that this combination of elevating off the ground, and then very physically clapping and stamping our feet, effects a drawing down of blessings from on high into this physical reality, and this paves the way to draw down holy souls of future children into this world.

The birth of new—whether it is new life as a couple or new souls being brought down into the world—requires a letting go of the old, and a general release of ego. The Frierdiker Rebbe teaches that joy and humility go hand in hand. Dancing is a way to let the joy penetrate even the body, and let go of oneself, and thus dancing with the bride or groom can help facilitate the perfect union, drawing down tremendous blessings into their new reality.

One of the very traditional forms of dancing, spoken of in the Talmud, is dancing in a circle. During the course of the wedding festivities there is a special mitzvah to dance "in front of the bride."

Circle dancing in front or around the bride is a mirror reflection of the circling of the bride around the groom during the chuppah.

The progression of the *Shefa*/abundant flow of blessings from on High, is that first the blessings are formed in the spiritual realm and then drawn down into the physical world. During the chuppah, the spiritual part of the wedding ceremony, the groom stands in the middle and the bride circles him, and during the physical celebration—the festive meal and the dancing—the bride is stationary and the groom with the other men dance in a circle. The groom and the bride also represent the spiritual and the physical, standing stationary represents the column of blessings that is being drawn down and encircling represents the maintaining of these blessings within this sacred space of the marriage, preventing negativity from entering this holy sphere.

Another traditional form of dancing, as spoken about by the Baal Shem Tov and his student the Maggid of Mezritch, is the "back and forth" dancing. In the circle, all the dancers move to the farthest reaches of the circle and then they all move together towards the middle, until they are face to face with each other, before moving back towards the outer part of the circle. This back and forth movement continues throughout the entire dance.

(For those familiar with it, the popular "Mayim" Israeli dance is danced this way. Juggling acts at wedding celebrations also date back to the sages of the Talmud, and juggling too is a back and forth, up and down movement).

This type of dancing and juggling is symbolic of marriage, where two people who have lived separate lives until now, with separate upbringings and genetic makeup, now choose to enter into a sacred covenant of union. They begin this "dance" at a distance from each other and then are drawn together in unity. Throughout the marriage there is this subtle dance between recognizing, acknowledging and honoring the otherness of one's spouse—giving the other their space—and the desire to unify and meld as one. It is a continuous back and forth, the dance of marriage.

Following the first set of dancing is the meal, which is considered a "*Seudat Mitzvah,*" a feast that is a mitzvah to partake of, and therefore there is a washing and reciting of "*HaMotzi*" on a festive challah.

The dancing and celebrations continue, and at the conclusion of the wedding, the *Bentching*/grace after meal is said together over a cup of wine, followed by another round of the *Sheva Berachot*/seven blessings.

SHEVA BERACHOT
The Seven Blessings

Every major life transition, both joyous and sad, is marked by a week
—one full cycle of creation—in which to fully incorporate the
new reality and move forward into the future.

Getting married is a major life change, and to honor this, the entire week following the wedding is set aside for the couple to be sequestered alone and enjoy their new life as a couple, and also for celebrations with the bride and groom that extend the joy of the wedding into the week that follows it.

The bride and groom are accompanied by a *Shomer*/a person who is designated to escort them when they leave the house, for just as a king and queen,
they should not be out unaccompanied for the week after the wedding.

For the entire week, friends and relatives host festive meals in honor of the new couple,
always inviting a *Panim Chadashot*, a new guest, who has not yet
celebrated with the couple.

These festive meals are called *Sheva Berachot*, referring to the
seven blessing that are recited after each of these meals.

www.ingramcontent.com/pod-product-compliance
Lightning Source LLC
LaVergne TN
LVHW070059080426
835508LV00028B/3457